CONTENTS

01 Notes

02 Introduction

03 The Basics: Why tiny changes make a big difference

04 How to create better habits to achieve anything you want

05 The basics to a better and more sustainable lifestyle

06 Eliminate or minimise your plastic consumption

07  Reduce the amount of wasted food

Leftovers are your best friends **08**

09  How to reduce plastic when doing groceries

Vintage shopping is the new cool **10**

11  The power of creating habits to become more sustainable and the best version of yourself

Sustainable product recommendations for the house to replace plastic options by room **12**

13 Takeaways and resources

Notes

- This guide aims to describe the processes through which one can create improved habits to better themselves. It is not solely focused on how to be more sustainable, but more so on how to normalize sustainability and integrate it as part of your everyday routine, as it is a more ethical way of life.

- Our entire concept is based on the philosophy of leading a more optimized lifestyle, to achieve our desires in life; namely a stable income, security of money, a home, being clothed and fed, etc... However, we need to improve our mindsets and our practices in order to become the best versions of ourselves.

- Part of the guide is inspired by Atomic Habits and The Miracle morning books. The fundamental keys to implementing habits such as these, is to adopt routines and habits that create a good lifestyle. Those sustainable habits + well-being habits + working on themselves is the greatest thing ever!

- This is an interactive guide, so feel free to make notes, write on it, use the QR codes to access exclusive materials and more! You should read it in order, but I encourage you to back and revisit sections if you need it. You can also use it as your go-to source of information when you are hesitant or need to know more about something specific.

Introduction

Hello dear reader! Welcome to the No Bullshit Guide to Sustainable & Effective Habits!

The fact you are reading this guide right now means you are open to new ideas and ready to make positive changes. Before we dive into the juicy stuff, I would like to take this opportunity to introduce myself and share my personal journey.

My name is Maria and back in 2020 at the start of the pandemic, a very close friend of mine and I began a conversation about the current global climate crisis and exploring the option of going zero waste. We started researching statistics regarding plastic pollution, food waste, carbon emissions... only to find the discovered information to be very alarming! Therefore, we decided we needed to be the change, in order to make a change.

We began looking into the best options and alternatives that we could implement in order to make such changes; soon realising that some of them were difficult to follow whilst living in the city, and the others were hard to stick to in the long term. I started an open discussion with many of my peers, and I realised that it was in fact a common problem! Many of them perceived being sustainable as somewhat of a challenge, costly and time-consuming.

That was the moment I realised I needed to do something about it! There was no way I was gonna let this go! I figured I needed to create something that was going to help guide people on this journey, with a method that was based on building habits they can not only apply to being more sustainable, but also to utilise in building whatever habits they wanted. For me, it was of the utmost importance to provide solutions and recommendations that people could integrate into their lifestyles. Instead of giving up aspects of their current lifestyle to be sustainable, they could integrate sustainability into their existing ones instead. Another key point I wanted to consider was that we, as humans, like comfort... so we might as well work with it and not against it!

Buckle up for the journey you are about to embark on. I hope you enjoy the ride!

1. The Basics: Why tiny changes make a big difference

> "Whether psychologically or physically, once a habit has been reinforced through enough repetition, it can be difficult to change. This is if you don't have an effective proven strategy"
>
> - Hal elrod, Miracle Morning Book

Whether it is exercising regularly, building a business, writing an essay or achieving any other goals one has set, we convince ourselves that massive success requires massive action; but have you ever considered the impact of making a minor adjustment or improvement a little more everyday?
A slight difference in your habits can lead your life's trajectory to an entirely different destination.

The same applies for creating sustainable habits. It is not about doing everything you are supposed to do all at once, but rather about adopting small changes that fit into your lifestyle and constructing new habits that work for you. Mastering individual habits will allow you to change your lifestyle, to become more sustainable, save more money, start that business... this is it, affirm and manifest to accomplish anything you want, if you just put your mind to it!

2. How to create better habits to achieve anything you want

The goal of this section: Based on the method used in the book "Atomic Habits" by James Clear we are going to explain how to create good habits, so you may achieve your goals.

This is going to set the base to explain how sustainable habits are going to become part of our routine because we are going to train our brain to unconsciously choose that over the unsustainable option, just because it's the right thing to do.

> "We often expect progress to be linear, fast and easy. It's important to understand that progress takes time, it's not linear and it can sometimes be frustrating. With time, we then realize everything we have accomplished"
>
> - Maria Grande

Create a routine: Consistency is key to forming solid habits and an improved attitude. The goal is to automate actions so you don't have to think twice as you do them. Your brain is familiar with that automation, so the level of effort the actions require becomes less over time.

Below is an interactive section for the purpose of the reader:

My morning routine is going to be:
Step 1:
Step 2:
Step 3:

My evening routine is going to be:
Step 1:
Step 2:
Step 3:

Achieving all your goals in one go isn't realistic: Creating healthier habits and routines can be time-consuming. Don't expect to accomplish everything you want within the first week. The initial stages will always be the easiest, but thereafter, consistency and willpower is the key to keeping that momentum.

This week I've achieved:

1. _____
2. _____
3. _____

Focus less on the goal and more on the system: Setting short and long term goals is important. They give one direction and focus for the road ahead. However, without a thought out system on how to achieve them, those goals are merely passing thoughts.

My goals are:

1.
2.
3.

Create positive cues that will trigger good habits: Imagine the process of disposing of trash, for instance; If your garbage bins are organized through a color system, your brain will automatically detect where the item has to go. This practice makes the habit of recycling a more efficient process.

List your cues and habits below: For example; When throwing something in the bin, I'm going to throw it in the right bin. For that, I am going to make notes of what goes in each bin.

When I	I'm going to	For that I'm going to
When I	I'm going to	For that I'm going to
When I	I'm going to	For that I'm going to

How to create more sustainable habits: The method:

(The following methods can be applied across the board and works for any habit you want to create)

Implementing this process successfully, starts with awareness. We need to start by identifying which of our current habits are unfavorable, and which are positive.

List them in the chart below:

Bad habits (To eliminate)	Good habits (To embrace)

The purpose of these exercises is to train our brains to reinforce positive actions, so that when A happens, B follows. With enough practice, we develop habits our brain instantly recognises and therefore, become automatic.

Once the list has been completed, we can proceed to the next step, which is identifying new habits we want to develop over time:

1. Make it obvious:

Examples are as follows; (i.) After I get out of bed in the morning, I will drink a glass of water, make coffee and have a stretch session (ii.) When I'm doing groceries, I will look for plastic-free alternatives first. (iii.) Before I get out of the house, I will make sure I always have a reusable bag with me, in case I buy anything.

Now it's your turn, create your new habits below:

1. After I .... I will ....
2. After I .... I will ....
3. After I .... I will ....

Note: Your environment plays a big role in the development of habits. The easier it is for us to do something, the more likely it is to occur. Find positive ways to make things easier for yourself.

For example, follow sustainable product accounts on social media platforms of your choice, such as Instagram or Facebook. This can help as one would see their content regularly, granting easy and consistent access to tips and information.

Other potential options could be having your recycling bins be easily accessible, finding various apps that deliver sustainable food alternatives to your doorstep, and many more... Bad habits are created because people instinctively gravitate towards what is convenient.

We tend to prefer staying within that comfort zone, rather than expanding our horizons and practices towards doing what in actuality, is better for us. Changing environments and fighting old habits or cues will become a lot easier, when consistently reinforcing the healthier habits.

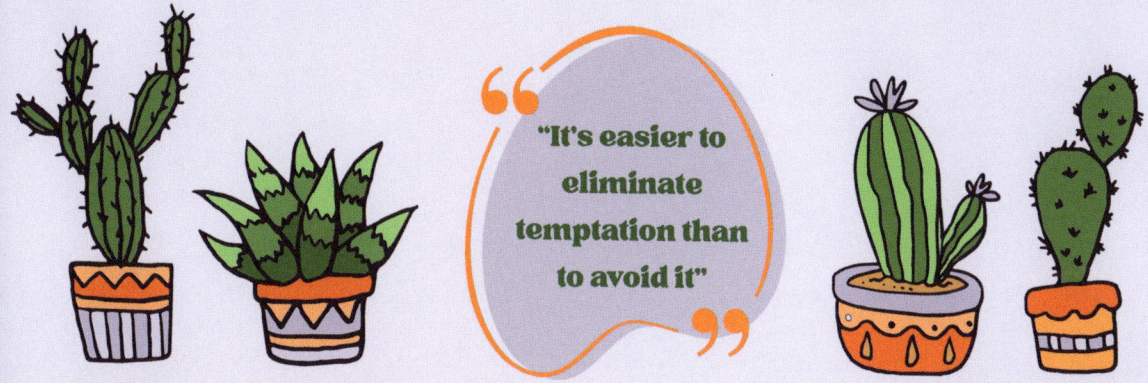

"It's easier to eliminate temptation than to avoid it"

2. Make it attractive: Dopamine

Incentives are what drives us to take action. The more attractive the reward is, the more likely we are to take that action. However, there is a slight issue with this; If the reward is not instant, we tend to get demotivated and are not as enthusiastic to complete the intended action.

Did you know, that friends and family, including general society, play a role in your developing habits? Yes, that's right. We tend to mirror habits that others may do around us, even habits that may be broadly approved by society or the majority... but guess what? It's about time you focus on yourself and your own intrinsic beliefs. What do you want to achieve, who do you want to become, how can you become more sustainable?

Dopamine drives our decisions. We long for that instant satisfaction, but good rewards can take time. We can give ourselves little rewards along the way to keep our motivation going, but the real results will come with time and consistent effort. The secret is to not let ourselves become demotivated and stagnate along the way.

3. Make it easy

The most effective form of learning is practice, not planning. Setting goals and a plan of action on how to achieve them is imperative, but the most important part of developing good habits is by actually doing them. Practice makes perfect, and even if you don't do it properly every time, your brain will start to pick the habit. Behavior becomes more progressive and begins to automate through repetition of the actions.

4. Make it satisfying

We tend to repeat behavior more often, when the experience is satisfactory and/ or enjoyable. To develop positive habits and stick to them, one needs to feel an immediate sense of success, even if the incentives are in minor ways. By making a habit satisfying, we are more likely to repeat it the next time.

For this exact reason, the principle of personalisation is so important. An experience that is satisfying for one, may not be as satisfying for another. It is important to find one's own way of enjoying the processes, whatever they may be; It could range from an exercise routine, to sustainable grocery shopping, writing that essay, recycling or any variety of activity. Find ways to find excitement in them or they become increasingly difficult to follow in the long term.

This is a trial and error process, as not everything will be perfect the first go around. Try something, if it doesn't work modify something and keep trying until you make that new habit enjoyable. Habit trackers and other visual forms of measurement can make your habit satisfying by providing clear evidence of your progress.

Let's start with the exercise below: For example; When able to recycle for 1 week straight, I will treat myself to something I like as a reward for completing the task.

When	I'm going to
When	I'm going to
When	I'm going to

Set this before you start working on the new habit, that way you have an additional positive and exciting new benefit to look forward to, in turn increasing motivation and consistency.

NOTES

*IMPORTANT! Set goals for yourself and rewards for accomplishing them. Keep yourself motivated to strive to achieve more!

3. The basics to a better and more sustainable lifestyle

> *"Instead of trying to achieve all your habits at once, go one by one. Once you master one, move onto the next"*

Goal of this section: Make changes that are going to become part of your daily routine. Habits that are going to become routine for you. Include old vs new triggers; for example, the old you would dispose of all trash items together, in the same container, however, the new you separates trash to recycle, using the appropriate disposal channels.

Our goals with this guide are

- Help you reduce the amount of waste you generate.
- Help you eliminate and or minimize your plastic consumption.
- Help you make better choices overall.
- Find alternatives to highly contaminating and non sustainable products.

"Sometimes, we'll rather choose being lazy than what is good for us, to make us better, for our future selves"

Description:

We understand that adopting sustainable habits can be challenging. It can be costly and may be perceived as time consuming. In this section we are getting started with simple changes to your daily habits that will assist in transforming your routine for the better, one small step at a time!

Now that we know how to develop habits, let's dive into how one can develop easy and simple sustainable habits that fit into your lifestyle.

You will need:

a. Two different marked trash cans or boxes to recycle at home.
b. Reusable shopping bags, as opposed to disposable plastics.
c. Optional: A DIY kit that can include sewing needles and thread, paint to repurpose packaging, etc…
d. A "Can do" attitude. You got this!

Steps to follow: The 5 Rs Principle

1. Reduce

The goal of this section is to reduce the amount of waste we create at home, resulting from packaging, food and various other sources. In order to reduce overall waste, we should aim to minimise the amount of product packaging we buy, as well as, the amount of wasted / unused food by making it last longer or giving it another use before throwing it away, and buying only what we need.

Some methods of waste reduction practices are listed below:

- Gradually eliminating single-use plastic consumption.
- Be wary of the amount of products you buy, keeping in mind that we live in a consumerist world. We don't need everything we buy, therefore considering what we actually require before making purchases can make all the difference.
- Controlling the amount of food waste we generate on a daily basis, be it cooked, uncooked or unused. Organising food better in the fridge, using the items by order of priority. Take into consideration what could potentially be repurposed, before deciding to dispose of it permanently.
- Taking into account the amount of packaging we consume everytime we buy something.

How are you going to start on your waste reduction journey?
List below the new habits you are going to create:

a. When I make orders through food delivery channels, I will make a note on the app, requesting the restaurant not to include disposable cutlery.

b. When I make orders through food delivery channels, I will keep the plastic containers at home, instead of throwing them out and instead, repurpose them. For example, to store my jewellery, dry food items, etc...

c. I will repurpose candle containers once the candle is done, as pen holders.

> "The old you would dispose of all trash items together, in the same container, however, the new you separates trash to recycle, using the appropriate disposal channels."

Now try yours by listing them below:

(Remember not to tackle too much at the same time. You need to master 1 or 2 habits initially, before going on to master others. We don't want to be overwhelmed and find ourselves unable to keep up.)

1.
2.
3.

ii. Recycle

Go to www.londonrecycles.com to see the recycling options in your area/building and read how to recycle at home. Find out more about recycling by postcode with https://londonrecycles.co.uk/recycling-services/ .

Recycling 101

Recycling Locator

How to recycle:

- Sort trash into two different types of containers; a general waste container and a recyclables container.
- Additionally, you could keep a third container, for things such as coffee pods, which can be recycled with your next coffee delivery (Depending on the brand, for instance, I personally give them to the delivery guy).
- Thinking this change may give you more work? Well, think again, because it doesn't! It takes the bare minimum!
  - How do we make this a habit? When you throw your trash at home, train your brain to throw your trash in the correspondent space, and a different container in the trash location.
  - Wash and fold your cartons before disposing of them or it may compromise the entire recycling process.
- It's that simple and easily implementable! Some people may find it difficult at the beginning, but we are creating a new habit so remember... In approximately 30 days, your efforts will no longer be such conscious actions, but rather an automatic part of your daily routine!

Separate your trash at home so it's easier for the recycling facility to recycle it for you. Separate paper from plastic and food waste. Take your electronics and other recyclables such as batteries to special recycling points.

BENEFITS:
- Protects the environment
- Less waste goes to landfill
- Saves energy

PAPER — PLASTIC — ORGANIC — BATTERY

INGRAIN STORE | 13   The no Bullshit guide to Sustainable & Effective Habits

Plastic:

According to Londonrecycles, these are some of the rules and guides you can follow.
If you live in a house or flat a within a house, your service may include:

Recycling
Black box | Collected once a week | Commercial areas - collections vary from weekly to twice daily

Recycling
Clear sack | Collected once a week | Commercial areas-collections vary from weekly to twice daily

Rubbish
Black sacks | Collected twice a week | Commercial areas - up to three times a day

Recycling
Black communal bins wih green lid | Collections vary from daily to weekly

Recycling
Green chutes | Collections vary from daily 10 weekly

Rubbish
Black communal bins | Collections vary from three times a week to daily

Food waste recycling (outdoors)
Larger black caddy with brown lid | Collected weekly

If you live on an estate or in a flat with communal bins, your service may include...

Rubbish
Underground Pod

Recycling
Dark green communal bin

Recycling
Underground pod

Rubbish
Metal communal bin with black lid

Recycling
Bleck communal bins wah green lid | Collections vary from daily to weekly

Recycling
Green chutes | Collections vary from daily to weekly

Rubbish
Black communal bins | Collections vary from three times a week to daily

Rubbish
Black chutes | Collections vary from three times a week to daily

Food waste:

- Brown bag/bin, keep it separate from the rest of your trash.
- Throw it in the food waste recycling can that is outside of your house/ flat.
- Do not mix your organics with the rest of your trash as it will contaminate the rest of the recyclables in the bag, and therefore they won't be able to be industrially recycled.
- Rinse packaging – leftover food residue can ruin your recycling.
- Leave labels on but remove plastic film and chuck it in your rubbish bin.

Food waste recycling
Brown small bin | Collected Monday, Wednesday and Friday

Food waste recycling
Green small bin | Collected Monday, Wednesday and Friday

Recycling symbols explained:

Widely recycled
This label is applied to packaging that is collected by 75% or more of local authorities across the UK, for example plastic bottles.

Widely recycled - rinse
Rinsing packaging, for example food trays, ensures that any food residue doesn't contaminate other materials, particularly if they are collected together with paper.

It also helps to stop attracting vermin into the recycling sorting centres where people work.

Not currently recycled
This symbol shows that less than 20% of local councils currently collect this packaging for recycling

The Green Dot
The Green Dot doesn't mean that the packaging is recyclable, will be recycled or has been recycled. It's a symbol used on packaging in some European countries and means the producer has made a financial contribution towards the recovery and recycling of packaging in Europe.

Mobius Loop
This means an item can technically be recycled but not that it has been recycled or that it will be accepted for recycling. Sometimes this symbol is used with a percentage figure in the middle to explain that the packaging contains x% of recycled material.

Plastic resin codes
This tells you what kind of plastic an item is made of.

INGRAIN STORE | 15   The no Bullshit guide to Sustainable & Effective Habits

Glass recycling
This symbol simply asks you to recycle the glass container.

Recyclable aluminium
This symbol indicates that an item is made from recyclable aluminium.

Recyclable steel
This symbol means that the product is made of steel. All councils collect steel for recycling!

Tidyman
This symbol from Keep Britain Tidy asks you not to litter.

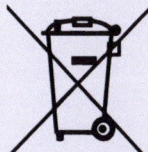

Waste electricals
This symbol explains that you should not place the electrical item in the general waste. Electrical items can be recycled through a number of channels.

Compostable
Products certified to be industrially compostable might have this 'seedling' logo. Never put compostable plastics into your recycling or food waste recycling bin.

Home composting
This symbol means that you can compost that item at home.

Paper, card and wood
The Forest Stewardship Council (FSC) logo means that in item has been made using wood from well managed forests.

Recycling Notes

NOTES

*IMPORTANT! Set goals for yourself and rewards for accomplishing them. Keep yourself motivated to strive to achieve more!

Hacks:

Hack #1
Keep a basket under the stairs or by the front door, to store your papers/magazines in before taking them to your outdoor recycling bin.

Hack #2
If you have kids, get them to decorate a plastic or cardboard box to store your recycling – not only will it brighten up your bin area, it'll encourage them to use it too!

Hack #3
Use bags for life to store bottles for recycling. Hang them on the inside of a kitchen cupboard door or in utility cupboards out of sight.

Hack #4
Store an old bucket under the sink to put your cans, glass and plastic in after you've rinsed them out.

Hack #5
Reuse cardboard wine carriers to store glass bottles neatly for recycling.

Now it's your turn, the list below will contain the new habits you are going to create. How are you going to reduce?:

a. I'm going to buy another bin or a recycling bin and put it in the kitchen, so that I can separate my trash more easily.

b. I'm going to put a paper on top of the bin to describe everything I can throw in there so I know where to throw my trash.

List yours below:
1.
2.
3.
4.
5.
6.

Reuse
- Clothes: Give them another life. Fix them. Repurpose them. Give them to a friend or family member.
- Packaging. You can use it for something else and even DIY to make it look better. (for example, store fruit, store jewellery, etc...)
- If you get any plastic packaging or bags, make sure you reuse them, that way they are not single use anymore (but you should still try to avoid plastic packaging)
- Leftovers. Who said leftovers can't be turned into a new dish! Is time to get creative here. The goal? Do not waste any of your leftovers.

Regrow

Vegetables. This is how you do it:

- <u>Onions</u>: Leave 1 in(2.5cms) of the onion and put it in water for 3-4 days. When it starts to grow white roots, put it in soil, cover it with more soil and water it. Take care of your onion until you have a new one (some recommend drying the onion before putting it in water).

The same applies for all veggies. Just leave the end where the roots are in water (top of the veggie can't be submerged in water so some people use toothpicks to help with this) until roots appear, then put in soil.

- <u>Potatoes</u>: Make sure there is 1-2 eyes on each half of a potato. Cut the potato in half and let sit overnight or until it's dry to touch. Plant halves one foot apart in 8 inches of soil.

- <u>Green onions</u>: Slice of the ends of the bulbs, leaving the roots attached. Put the bulb's root in a small jar submerged in water (only the root). Replace water daily. Sprouts should pop up within 3 days.

How to regrow veggies with water links:

Gardening know how website

Don't waste the crumbs website

Herbs. This is how you do it:

A little sprinkle of fresh herbs on a meal can mean the difference between flavours that are just nice, and flavours that are spectacular. When you have your own herbs, it makes it easier to boost the flavour of your homemade meals.

Growing a herb garden of your own and having a fresh supply of these aromatics, is the perfect gardening project for spring. However, before getting started you'll want to learn about the best growing conditions, decide on a gardening method that will work for you, and think about whether you want to start with seeds or live plants.

The good news about herbs is that they don't need to be grown in a garden; almost any kitchen can accommodate pots or window boxes, and with the right care and attention, your herbs will flourish.

It's best to go easy on yourself and start by planting pre-potted herbs. You can get them in garden centres and most supermarkets, and they'll save you loads of time and energy. Aim to plant your herbs in April or early May when there's no frost.

Quick links you can use for your herbs:

Eatingwell.com

Cnet.com

Goodhousekeeping.com

Benefits: Also unmatched flavour for a fraction of the cost of their grocery-store counterparts.

Jamieoliver.com

Cookinglight.com

Gerdenerspath.com

Scan me with your phone

Rot

- This might be one of the hardest steps to follow, given that London doesn't have too many compost locations around the city.
- Possible things you can do to compost are put all of your organic food waste together in a trash bag or container that you can freeze. Because it's frozen it won't smell or cause you any trouble.
- Once you are ready to take it to your local garden, which you can do once a month. You can find the different compost locations on www.londonrecycles.com.

TIPS

- Start by noting down everything you throw away and all the packaging you collect in a week to understand your waste and the areas where you need to improve.
- Everything starts with small steps, so don't try to do everything at once, or else you can feel overwhelmed and give up. Practice makes perfect and is better to do something than not do anything at all.

4. Eliminate or minimise your plastic consumption

> "Perfection can only be achieved if people, companies and governments collaborate as one. However, that doesn't mean your contribution doesn't help to fight climate change. everything you do counts, everything your friends and family do count. We just need to start!"

Description:

Plastic is one of the worst things for the planet! It takes a very long time to decompose, and some of them don't fully disappear... It breaks down over around 500 years becoming microplastics, which are then eaten by fish... and yeah, you guessed it... us humans as well.
Here is an example of plastic types and how long they take to decompose (WWF, 2021).

You will need:

- A pen and a notepad

Steps to follow:

Make a list of the amount of plastic you consume in 3 -5 days to understand your consumption. List them below

a.
b.
c.

Where can you eliminate or minimise plastic, for which items? List them below:

a.
b.
c.

Now adopt those products over the plastic options for a week. Did you notice any changes?

Update your plastic consumption after product swaps below:

a.
b.
c.
d.
e.
f.

Make a list of possible uses of the plastic containers you have so that it's easier for you to use. Pen holder? Plant pot? Or perhaps a food container to store food at home? You can use plastic cutlery from your takeaway order at the house and reuse it as much as you can (Make sure you recycle the plastic you throw away).

The possibilities are endless! List the uses below as a reminder for you:

a.
b.
c.
d.
e.
f.

Plastic that you can't recycle at home (they need to be industrially recycled therefore they need to go into the rubbish bin). Examples include:

- Crisp packets
- Sweet wrappers
- Plastic film
- Laminated pouches
- Medicine blister pack
- Polystyrene
- Plastic toys (hard plastics)
- Plastic bottles containing chemicals
- Squeeze toothpaste tubes
- Nappies
- Bubble wrap
- Plastic bags
- Plastic bottles

List of products with hidden plastic:

- Micro fiver clothes
- Some takeaway items
- Microfiber cleaning cloths
- Drink cartons
- Envelops
- Wet wipes
- Sponges
- Teabags (the ones that are not rippable contain plastic)
- Takeaway coffee cups (They look like paper on the outside but still contain plastic)
- Water bottles
- Face masks
- Liquid and cream containers
- Drink cans (they have an epoxy shield)
- Glass jars with plastic lids or straws
- Tetra Packs
- Tin/Aluminium cans (They are lined with plastic)
- Foil packaging (e.g. snack bars, chip bags,...)
- Paper or cardboard food and drink packaging (it contains plastic)
- Disposable wipes
- Paper containing plastic
- Chewing gum
- Clothing
- Glass jars with lids
- Glitter
- PLAs and Corn-Based Biodegradable Packaging
- Packaging stickers
- Shower curtains

These are just some examples I wanted to include in the guide, but the list goes on...

- If you are going to buy something that has plastic packaging, think twice when you buy it. Do you really need to buy it in that format? Or can you find a different more sustainable format? Can you get something else instead?

- For example, if I want to buy a pack of Oreos that comes in a plastic container I can instead get another snack that comes in paper packaging instead. Often various options are available to us, so we have the opportunity to make smart choices.

- When you are ordering food from apps such as Deliveroo and Ubereats, make a note on the order to specify you don't want any cutlery. If you get any by mistake, keep it at home and reuse it as many times as possible.

NOTES

IMPORTANT! Set goals for yourself and rewards for accomplishing them. Keep yourself motivated to strive to achieve more!

5. Reduce the amount of wasted food

> "Sometimes we think that going out of our way requires too much effort, but we don't realise that is a tiny change with a small amount of effort required"

Description:

Let's face it.. we've all been there. We forgot to use those vegetables in the fridge, eat that piece of fruit or eat those leftovers that have been sitting on the fridge for over a week now... Not to worry! This section will help you repurpose and remind yourself how to make the most out of the food you have at home.

According to the UK government, the UK throws around 9.5 tonnes of waste each year (As of 2018), 60% of those coming from households (UK Parliament, 2021).

You will need:

- A pen and a notepad

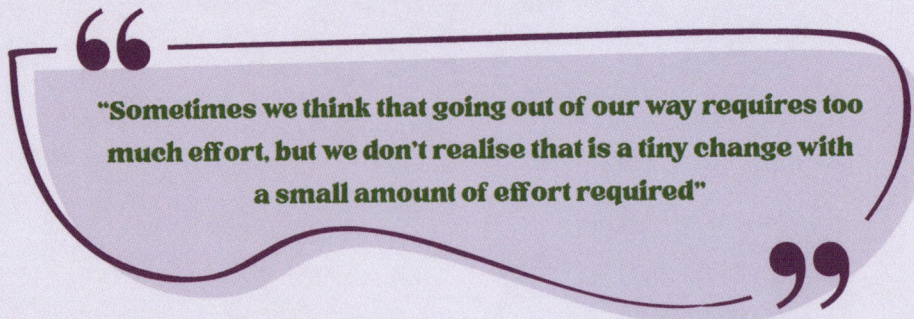

Steps to follow:

- In your notebook, note down the amount of food you throw into the bin before it's used. Do this for a week so you can understand your areas for improvement.

Best ways to keep vegetables for longer at home: (Zerowastechef, 2017)

Asparagus: Store at room temperature in a glass of water with the stems down. The asparagus will keep for over a week. Change the water mid-week.

Avocado: Store at room temperature until ripe and then transfer to the refrigerator to store. If you eat only half of an avocado, store the other half in the refrigerator with the pit in. It will last longer.

Basil: Storage in the refrigerator can brown the leaves and speed up basil's demise. Store it at room temperature with stems placed in a jar of water. Large bunches can double as a centrepiece.

Beets: Greens draw moisture out of root vegetables. Remove them and store separately in the refrigerator for up to a few days. Store the beets in the crisper drawer for up to 10 days.

Bell pepper: Store these in a cool place, however, cold temperatures in the refrigerator can cause them to break down faster. If you don't have a cool spot for storage, in the refrigerator peppers will last for a few days.

Bok choy: Store in the refrigerator for up to a week in a cloth produce bag.

Broccoli: Broccoli perishes quickly. Store it in the refrigerator in a cloth produce bag and eat within three or four days.

Brussels sprouts: Like broccoli, brussels sprouts perish quickly. Store them in the refrigerator in a cloth produce bag and eat within a few days.

Cabbage: Store loose in the crisper drawer and use within about two weeks.

Carrots: Remove the greens and store in the refrigerator in a cloth produce bag or loose in the crisper drawer. They will keep for a week or longer.

Cauliflower: Store this loose in the refrigerator on the crisper drawer. Use it within a week.

Celery: The best way to store it is in water (change the water mid-week). Or store your celery in the refrigerator (in a cloth bag if you prefer).

Corn: Within hours of being picked, corn loses up to 40 percent of its sugar. Eat it as soon as you buy it. If you must store it, put it in a warmer part of the refrigerator in the husk for up to three days.

Cucumber: The refrigerator is too cool for these and can damage the texture. They last longer if kept outside the fridge. If you do store them in the refrigerator, eat them within a few days.

Dark leafy greens: —chard, collards, kale and spinach—. Remove the stems, cut, wash and spin dry in a cloth produce bag (do this outside). Store them in the same now-damp but not wet cloth produce bag. Use them up within a week.

Eggplant: Store at room temperature. Colder temperatures can damage them. They will keep for about a week.

Green beans: These perish quickly so gobble them up soon after buying. Store them in a cloth produce bag in the refrigerator for about three days. Cut off the stem only, not the edible end. This reduces waste and saves time.

Herbs: Store in cloth produce bags in the refrigerator for up to a week (except for basil).

Hot peppers: Like bell peppers, hot peppers do better outside of the refrigerator. Store jalapeños, poblanos and serrano chiles at room temperature. If you will use them within a few days, you can keep them in the refrigerator.

Lettuce: Store lettuce in the refrigerator. Cut, wash, spin, then store in a cloth produce bag in the refrigerator for up to a week.

Leeks: Store them in the refrigerator for up to two weeks.

Mushrooms: Store them in a cloth produce bag in the refrigerator. Use up these delicate fungi soon after purchase. Some varieties will keep for up to a week.

Onions and shallots: Store them in a cool, dry place but not in the refrigerator, as the cold temperature can damage the flavour and texture.

Potatoes: Store in a cool but not cold place and keep them away from ethylene producing fruit and strong-smelling garlic, onions and leeks, which can impart their flavours onto potatoes. Also, keep them away from light to avoid greening.

Pumpkin, winter squash: They don't do well in the refrigerator. Store at room temperature.

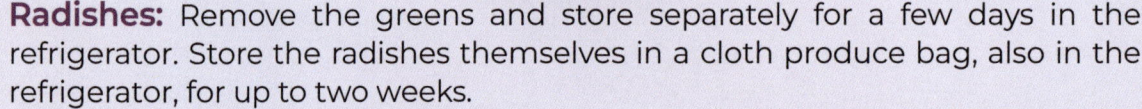

Radishes: Remove the greens and store separately for a few days in the refrigerator. Store the radishes themselves in a cloth produce bag, also in the refrigerator, for up to two weeks.

Root vegetables: Store beets, carrots, parsnips, rutabaga and turnips at cold temperatures in the refrigerator. If you have a root cellar, store them there for the long haul.

Scallions (aka green onions): Store them in a cloth produce bag in the refrigerator and use within a week.

Sprouts: If you make these yourself, wait until they have completely dried from their final rinse before you store them in either a cloth produce bag, glass jar or glass container. Store purchased sprouts in the same manner.
Summer squash (such as zucchini): This perishes quickly. Store in the refrigerator for up to several days.

Sweet potatoes: Like regular potatoes, store in a cool place but do not refrigerate.

Tomatoes: Store at room temperature. Do not refrigerate! Cold temperatures result in mealy tomatoes devoid of flavour.

Best ways to keep fruit for longer at home: (Zerowastechef, 2017)

Apples: Apples will keep for about a week at room temperature and longer in the refrigerator. In a cold cellar, they can keep for several months. They give off quite a bit of ethylene (except for Fuji and Granny Smith), so keep them away from other produce, unless you want that produce to ripen quickly, such as hard avocados, pears or Hachiya persimmons.

Bananas: Store them at room temperature and keep them away from everything else as they give off lots of ethylene and will speed up the demise of other produce (unless that produce isn't ripe and you want to ripen it)Cantaloupe and honeydew melons: Store them in a cool area but not a cold refrigerator. If you need to store half a melon (with the rind still on), leave the seeds in and store in the refrigerator, face down on a plate to prevent exposure to air.

Citrus: Store grapefruit, lemons, limes and oranges at room temperature for a couple of weeks. They can develop spots on the rind in the fridge.

Figs: Store them in the refrigerator in a glass container in a single layer to prolong them. Don't wash them until you're ready to eat them.

Grapes: Like most items in this list, these turn quickly. Store in a cloth produce bag and refrigerate for up to five days to prolong freshness.

Kiwis: If they're hard, store them in the refrigerator for up to a month and remove as desired to ripen. Once ripe—or if you bought them ripe—return them to the refrigerator for up to 10 days.

Pears: Store at room temperature until ripe and then move to the refrigerator where they will keep for several days.

Persimmons: Store both Hachiyas and Fuyus at room temperature. Eat Hachiyas when they have practically rotted (they taste delicious at that point)

Pomegranates: Store these in a cool but not cold place. Store seeds in a glass jar or glass container in the refrigerator for a few days.

Stone fruits: Highly perishable apricots, nectarines, peaches and plums will turn quickly so gobble them up while they're fresh. If you buy them hard, store them at room temperature until ripe, then transfer them to the refrigerator for up to several days.

Watermelon: Keep these at room temperature. Cold temperatures can damage their flesh, resulting in pitting and loss of colour and flavour. Watermelons are ethylene-sensitive, so keep them away from fruits that produce high amounts of ethylene.

Cantaloupe and honeydew melons: Store them in a cool area but not a cold refrigerator. If you need to store half a melon (with the rind still on), leave the seeds in and store in the refrigerator, face down on a plate to prevent exposure to air.

Cherries and berries: Cherries, blackberries, blueberries, raspberries and strawberries turn quickly so ideally, eat them the day you buy them. If you must wait, store them in the refrigerator in glass containers or a cloth produce bag for up to about five days. Don't cram them into giant jars or bags though or they'll bruise. Wash and stem them just before you eat them. They don't emit much ethylene.

Top habits and tricks to avoid food waste before it's wasted. How to revive poor looking produce:

- You can revive kale by cutting stems, putting them in water & into the fridge for a few hours.
- Revive carrots in the fridge overnight by peeling them and submerging them in water.
- Put strawberries with imperfections in cold water for 20 min and they come out as new.
- For most produce, you can submerge the food in a bucket or large bowl of ice water. Then, put the container with the vegetables in the fridge, to keep the water cool. Let the food soak for 15 to 30 minutes. Heartier produce, such as root vegetables, may need longer, or up to one hour.
- For foods with stalks, such as asparagus, broccoli and herbs, you may be able to treat them like flowers: put the ends of the produce in a jar of water, and let them soak. Just be sure to trim the ends a bit to open up the cells. You may have to let them soak a bit longer, but you'll save water.
- If you find food that is close to rotting or showing signs of rot, you've reached a point of no return. Produce that is also discoloured or covered in dark spots is also likely too far gone. Other obvious signs of decay include slimy texture, mould growth and liquefied portions. These foods should be trashed-or better yet, taken to your compost pile.

Tips:

- Reuse, reuse, reuse: Instead of throwing something away, think of giving it another life. Something you don't use? Ask friends and family if they want it, give it to someone who needs it or sell it!
- Wash berries in diluted vinegar and extend life up to 2 weeks.
- Store onions in old thighs and make them last up to 8 months.
- Carrots and celery submerged in water will last up to 1 month, celery up to 2 weeks.
- Have an eat me first side or basket in the fridge to prevent from wasting forgotten food.
- Leafy greens will last up to 10 days wrapped in a tea towel.
- Store potatoes with an apple to prevent sprouting.
- Raw ginger keeps for about 1 week at room temperature, 1 month in the fridge and up to 6 months in the freezer.

To keep your greens from spoiling too soon, first remove any tight bands or ties, then rinse and dry fully (these should not stay wet!) before wrapping loosely in a dry tea towel and placing uncrowded in the fridge.

Kale, a hardier green, will stay crisp and full when placed in a cup of water like a bouquet in the fridge.

Apple: Crisper drawer, up to 3 weeks.

Banana: Countertop, up to 3 days if ripped.

Melon: Stored in the fridge wrapped in reusable wrap, up to 10 days.

Tomatoes: Countertop, up to 5 days.

Avocado: Counter until ripe, then fridge. Up to 4 days in the fridge.

Cut avocado: Lemon juice on the cut side. Wrapped in reusable wax wrap. In the fridge for 1 day.

Lime: Fridge shelf. Up to 2 weeks.

Cut lime: Wrapped in reusable wax wraps in the fridge. Up to 3 days.

Store fruit and veggies separately to avoid spoiling too fast.

When you think about what to eat, go through your options in the fridge first in order of priority (products about to expire first, leftovers, etc...)

If there is something you didn't eat because you weren't too interested in them, don't buy it again.

There are a lot of **places you can get instant inspiration from** when you don't know when to cook.

You can even **order the food you want** and still use some of the ingredients at home to make a side dish or even elevate your dish.

Are you missing key ingredients for your recipe? Use a fast grocery delivery system that can get you the ingredients you are missing within 15-20 minutes like Getir, Gorilla, Deliveroo... use ones that use as less plastic packaging as possible.

6. Leftovers are your best friends

Description: Most people don't realise how much food they throw away every day, from uneaten leftovers to spoiled produce. EPA estimates that in 2018, about 68 percent of the wasted food we generated or in other terms, 42.8 million tons, ended up in landfills and combustion facilities (Businesswaste. 2022). By managing food sustainably and reducing waste, we can help businesses and consumers save money, provide a bridge in our communities for those who do not have enough to eat, and conserve resources for future generations.

Making sure we eat all of the food we prepare is an important way to reduce waste, conserve resources, and save money. Start showing your leftovers some love today.

> "I don't feel like eating what I ordered yesterday anymore... then use it to make something else!"

How to:

- **Create rules at home...** Make sure to eat your leftovers within 2-3 days; they are still delicious and it helps you to avoid cooking. Is the easiest way to avoid food going to waste.
- **Don't throw them out...** Whether you're eating at home or out at a restaurant, don't let leftover edible food go to waste in the trash or compost bin. No amount is too little to save when your hard-earned money and resources are on the line. Eating at a friend's house? Distribute the leftovers amongst everyone if the host can't keep them all.

- **At restaurants**, get a to-go box, or better yet, bring your own container... A lot of restaurants nowadays are adopting sustainable packaging for customers who want to take their leftovers home.

- **Just don't forget** it on the table when you leave. After a home-cooked meal, pack up the leftovers and get them into the fridge after everyone has filled up. Store them in a place in the fridge where you won't forget about them.
- **Saving leftovers** is a quick way to pack a low-effort lunch. Just pop them into the right-sized container, and you're ready to go! If there is not enough food for a full meal, pack an extra snack or aside.

Reinvent them...

Get creative in the kitchen. Leftover vegetables are easily combined or baked into new dishes. Reinvent grains and meats into fried rice, hash, scrambles, and soups. The web is filled with ideas on "what to do with extra ..."
You can find recipes for your leftovers in cookbooks, Instagram, Pinterest, Google,... or just get creative!

Freeze them...

If you like the food that's leftover but just don't want to eat more of it now or even this week, freeze it in portion sizes or family dinner sizes to consume later. You'll thank yourself when you have a busy schedule and no time to make a meal. Just be sure to label your container so you don't have a frozen mystery jar that requires an act of bravery to defrost.

Swap them...

Industrious folks have turned leftovers into a useful crowdsourcing hobby with group food swaps or dinner swaps. These groups or events consist of a few people making extra food and then swapping it to get more variety for their effort.

Prevent them...

If you really hate leftovers, make an effort to avoid them in the first place by matching the amount of food you cook or buy with the amount of food you eat. Use a portion calculator when you cook, especially if you're trying something new. If you are out at a restaurant and eating something that doesn't store well, split it with a partner or friend. You might even get bold and request a half-serving or smaller portion!

Other: Check out the "Too good to go" app to rescue food from your local restaurants at a cheaper price. Food that otherwise would go to waste.

Now is your turn, list your favourite leftover recipes below so you can have easy access to them, and all in one place for future reference:

1.
2.
3.

NOTES

*IMPORTANT! Set goals for yourself and rewards for accomplishing them. Keep yourself motivated to strive to achieve more!

7. How to reduce plastic when doing groceries

Description:

Single-use plastics come with a steep environmental price, one that we'll be paying off for millennia. Our plastic addiction is having a devastating impact on our oceans, our wildlife, and our health.

Single-use plastics are a glaring example of the problems with throwaway culture. Instead of investing in quality goods that will last, we often prioritise convenience over durability and consideration of long-term impacts.

Reducing plastic use is the most effective means of avoiding waste (and the impacts linked to plastic production and use).

Individual choices and the collective shifts they bring about, add up quickly. Making just one simple swap, can spare the environment from being polluted by hundreds of plastics each year. Here are a few more tips for ridding your life (and your community) of single-use plastics for good.

> "It's almost impossible to do groceries without a single plastic packaging from an everyday store, like Waitrosse and Tesco. What we can do instead is reduce the amount we get by making better choices"

How To:

- Avoid products with plastic packaging
- If you get anything plastic-based and it can be reused, clean it and repurpose it to use at home.
- Remember to take your own reusable bags to the store.
- If you forget your bag and you need to buy a plastic one at the store, reuse it at home to pack your lunch, take your shoes to work, another grocery run... make single-use plastic, no longer single-use.
- Buy fruits and veggies from the market, rather than from the store and take a bag for them. The farmers market will usually give you paper bags for the produce instead of plastic bags.
- Some useful apps to order more sustainable groceries from: Oddbox, too good to go...
- Buy bread from the bakery at the supermarket and ask for it to be in a paper bag or order from a local bakery. You can add a note on your order and ask for a paper bag instead of plastic.

Where and what plastic I got	How can I avoid it

Tips:

Make a list of sustainable shops you can use to buy your groceries online or at a store, so that when you need to buy something you have it handy and you don't have to overthink. Avoiding tedious troubles to make your habits more sustainable.

Mark as favourite your most beloved restaurants, that you know use sustainable takeaway packaging. That way when you order takeaway, the process becomes easier.

Our recommendations for the U.K. are: Shoreline Shaving, Salt Cup, Upcircle, your Local Farmers Market, Green Island...

Make your list of favourites here:

a.
b.
c.
d.
e.
f.

How to reduce plastic when ordering food:

1. Say no to cutlery.
2. If you get cutlery, reuse it at home so it's not single use anymore.
3. Make a list of restaurants that you like that use less plastic packaging and order from them!
4. Make a list of restaurants that use more plastic packaging.
5. Avoid the second list, and update them both as you go.
6. Reuse the plastic containers you get for food storage.

Restaurant that uses too much plastic	Alternatives

8. Vintage shopping is the new cool

Description:

Thrifting not only helps your wallet but also the planet! The fashion industry is one of the most polluting industries globally. It's a great way to deal with textile waste and save a little extra money. Second-hand clothes also help you feel and look great.

> "I used to think that buying second-hand clothes was not as good, but I've realised that's not the case. You can find amazing and beautiful pieces while saving £"

> "Buying just one white cotton shirt produces the same amount of emissions as driving 35 miles in a car."
> (Oxfam, 2021)

What are the environmental impacts of fast fashion? (Ovo energy, 2020)

Carbon Emissions: About 10% of the world's greenhouse gas emissions (including carbon) come from the fashion industry.

Water Usage: The fashion industry glugs approximately 1.5 trillion litres of water every year, and it's only expected to get worse. Without significant changes, if demand for fashion continues to grow at the same pace, the industry could be consuming 50% more water by 2030.

Polyester Fabrics: 70 million barrels of oil per year are used to make polyester fibres. Not only do these man-made fabrics use a lot of fossil fuels during the manufacturing process, but they're also impossible to get rid of, because they don't decay in the way that natural fibres do. In fact, the plastics in our clothes are one of the leading causes of the plastics in our oceans.

Toxic Textile Dyes: Bright, colourful clothing is great for making a statement – but have you ever thought about how those colours were created? Many fashion brands use chemical dyes that are toxic to our environment, and end up polluting rivers and oceans. This makes the fashion industry the second biggest polluter of water after the agriculture industry.

Waste: Three quarters of Brits throw away their old clothes, rather than donating or recycling them. Our culture of buying outfits just to wear them once, results in lots of fashion ending up in the bin.

Manufacturing in developing countries: Many western fashion brands pay for their clothes to be made in factories based in developing countries. This can mean that the resulting pollution is a lot higher in countries where regulations on manufacturing are less strict. It can also lead to exploitation of garment workers and other labourers, who are often paid less than a living wage, and face dangerous working conditions. While that's not directly an environmental issue, it does make the fashion industry less sustainable.

How to buy more sustainable:

- Vintage market shopping (Brick Lane, Shoreditch, Portobello). Online vintage shopping (Depop, Vinted, Vestiaire,...).
- Luxury vintage shopping (Depop, Vinted, Sellier Knightsbridge,
- Luxurypromise,...). Find out if there are things that someone in your family doesn't want anymore and ask for it.
- Donate it!
- Sell it. There are great platforms where you can do that, such as eBay,Depop,...
- Rent items for a special occasion.
- Make it yourself. There are plenty of tutorials on YouTube that teach you how to make your own clothes. If you are feeling adventurous you can try it yourself!
- Dead stock. If you would like to shop from a specific brand's sample collection this is for you. You can buy items that brands used as samples that would otherwise go to waste.
- Fix it. Remember that when something breaks you can fix it, when you don't like something you can DIY to make it look different and fresh or you can even donate it, but don't throw fashion items away unless they can't serve anymore. You can find a lot of DIY videos on Youtube as well.
- Sustainable brands. There are a lot of sustainable brands where you can buy items that don't carry a high price tag; for example, Tala, Swim Society...

Now it's your turn. Where would you like to start? List 3 options you want to try below:

1.
2.
3.

List your favourite stores below:

a.
b.
c.

d.
e.
f.

Do you want to give away clothes?

I'm going to give...   to.....
I'm going to give...   to.....
I'm going to give...   to.....

Notes: Use this section to organise your fashion habits every time you need to use it for something, and remember

SAY NO TO FAST FASHION. IF YOU ARE PAYING CHEAP, SOMEONE ELSE IS PAYING THE PRICE FOR YOU (WORKERS).

NOTES

*IMPORTANT! Set goals for yourself and rewards for accomplishing them. Keep yourself motivated to strive to achieve more!

9. The power of creating habits to become more sustainable and the best version of yourself

Description:

Being more sustainable and creating good habits is the best for you, as well as for the planet! It helps protect the environment and reduce overall waste. Living sustainably is an important practice to help in saving the environment and using our resources efficiently. Whether people have sustainable habits or just getting started, your individual practices can make all the difference.

It's important to remember that you don't have to set yourself up for failure. You have to find something that works for you... because nobody is perfect, and we are not expecting you to be. We are just trying to aid you in your journey to being as sustainable as you can be!

According to the book " Atomic Habits" by James Clear, creating habits is a matter of repetition, until the habit becomes automatic.

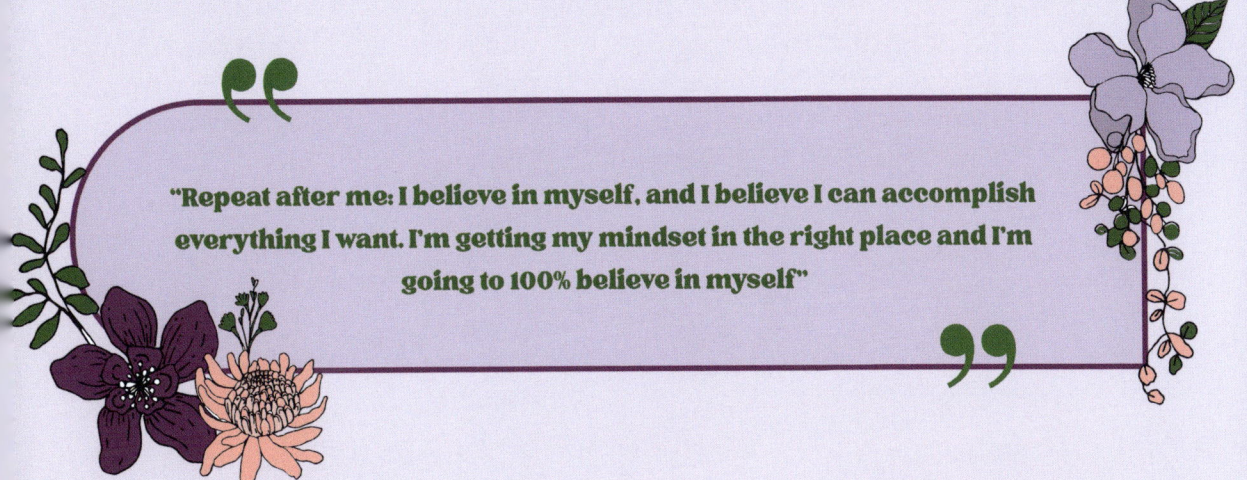

"Repeat after me: I believe in myself, and I believe I can accomplish everything I want. I'm getting my mindset in the right place and I'm going to 100% believe in myself"

Let's make your habits more sustainable.

How to:

- When I see plastic, I say no. I find alternatives.
- When I throw something in the trash, I think which is the correct bag to dispose of the item in. I recycle properly.
- When I order takeout, I reuse all the cutlery and containers as much as I can, even if they are wooden.
- Before going shopping, I ask myself, do I really need this item or am I going to tire of it soon?
- When I go shopping, I first look for plastic-free alternatives and quality options that will last me a longer time.

Now start creating your own in the section below:

When I... (Action)	I'm going to (Consequence/improvement)	My reward for it

The benefit of this process is that when you learn how to create a new sustainable habit, you are teaching yourself how to learn a new habit, which can be applied to any area of your life... going to the gym, your morning routine, how to be more productive and stay motivated, amongst many more.

Let's go a step further and list other habits you are looking to adopt in the long run. Remember that in order for it to work, you should master one before going into the next, and to remember that this is not about overcoming too much all at once. Our goal is 1% everyday.

Other habits I would like to adapt are:

1.
2.
3.

Remember to reward yourself when you achieve something. You did it! This also works great as motivation.

Tip: Instant gratification is not our friend. Results take time, but the reward and gratification will be much greater at the end. Remember that consistency will take you to places that motivation never will.

NOTES

*IMPORTANT! Set goals for yourself and rewards for accomplishing them. Keep yourself motivated to strive to achieve more!

10. Sustainable product recommendations for the house to replace plastic options by room

Description:

Buying good quality and sustainable products will help you save money in the long-run. Reusable alternatives made from metal or biodegradable materials are the best options, especially for things we use more often, as this will reduce our carbon footprint, as well as help you save money.

Below are some of our recommendations that you can get started with:

- Brush to clean dishes.
- Soap to clean dishes.
- Dishwasher pods.
- Silicone zip bags to avoid plastic containers : Green island.
- Bamboo toilet paper : Cheeky panda.
- Bamboo kitchen paper : Cheeky panda.
- Cloth to avoid kitchen paper which is single-use.
- Updircle beauty.
- Shampoo.
- Metal razor: Shoreline shaving.
- Menstrual cup: Saalt cup.
- Reusable straws: Green island.
- Reusable tea bags.
- Beeswax wrap.
- Water bottle.
- Compostable bin bag.
- Reusable shopping bag and net for produce.
- Coffee : Grind coffee.
- Compostable coffee cups: Grind coffee.
- Kitchen sponge: Green island.
- Soap to clean dishes: Green island.
- Bring your own bag : Anywhere.
- Rechargeable lighter
- Bamboo facial towel to clean and remove makeup: Upcirlce.
- House cleaners + refills: Cleandrop cleaners.

11. Takeaways

- It's not about being perfect, it's about making positive changes.
- Don't try and do more than you are able to. We are behavioural creatures, so building a new habit can take time; make sure you are comfortable with doing one constantly rather than overwhelming yourself, resulting in you throwing the towel, and giving up in the end. Discipline and consistency will take you to places that motivation cannot. Remember that.
- For me, being sustainable is not about changing your lifestyle and making it hard for yourself to follow those changes, it is about integrating good habits into your lifestyle that allow you to commit and stick to them, because it's the right thing to do for the future of the planet.
- Don't tackle and try to implement this guide all at once. Go through it at your own pace, section by section. Master one habit then move on to the next.
- Don't be naive in thinking that your new sustainable habits won't have a significant impact on the environment, because every little bit genuinely helps. Be the change you want to see in the world!

You are not alone! If you have questions or just require a little support on your journey, you can connect with me or Ingrain via the following links:

✉ Ingrainstore@gmail.com

📷 @ingrainstore

📷 @mariaeugeniagrande

Best of luck to you all and I hope to see you soon!

NOTES

*IMPORTANT! Set goals for yourself and rewards for accomplishing them. Keep yourself motivated to strive to achieve more!

Resources

Atomic Habits. Tiny changes remarkable results: James Clear
The Miracle Morning: The 6 Habits That Will Transform Your Life Before 8AM: Hal Elrod
London recycles, 2022, https://londonrecycles.co.uk
UK Parliament Food waste, 2021 - https://lordslibrary.parliament.uk/food-waste-in-the-uk/
The lifestyle of plastics. WWF Australia, 2021 - https://www.wwf.org.au/news/blogs/the-lifecycle-of-plastics
Fast fashion: what it is, why it's bad for the environment, and how to shop smarter, Ovo energy 2020 - https://www.ovoenergy.com/guides/energy-guides/how-fast-fashion-impacts-the-environment
Zero waste chef, 2017 - https://zerowastechef.com/2017/01/20/store-produce-without-plastic/
Food waste 2022: The facts. Zero waste chef, 2022 - https://www.businesswaste.co.uk/food-waste-2022-the-facts/
Business waste, 2022, https://www.businesswaste.co.uk/food-waste/
white cotton shirt quote: Oxfam 2021, https://www.oxfam.org.uk/about-us/private-sector/sustainable-fashion/

Copyright © Maria Grande 2022

This book is copyright material and must not be copied, reproduced, transferred, distributed, leased, licensed or publicly performed or used in any way except as specifically permitted in writing by the publishers, as allowed under the terms and conditions under which it was purchased or as strictly permitted by applicable copyright law. Any unauthorized distribution or use of this text may be a direct infringement of the author's and publisher's rights and those responsible may be liable in law accordingly.

Printed in Great Britain
by Amazon